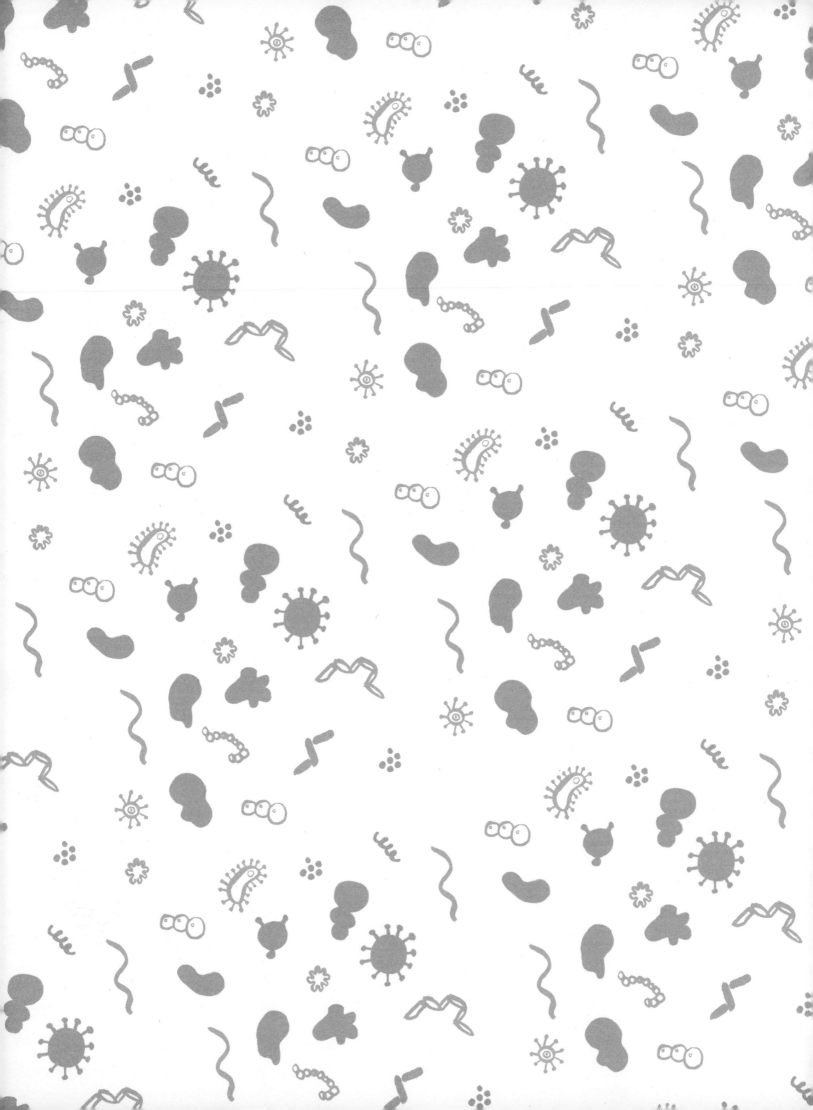

Gut Garden

Katie Brosnan

For my Mum, who started
off my microbiome
-
KB

WHAT ARE MICROBES?

Microbes are tiny life forms that you can only see with a microscope. They come in millions of shapes and sizes and they are EVERYWHERE. Every single habitat no matter how cold or hot or inhospitable has microbes.

These are the main categories of microbes that scientists have discovered:

There are 40 million bacterial cells in one gram of soil!

Bacteria

Bacteria are single-celled organisms that are neither plants nor animals. They can be found everywhere from glaciers to the depths of the ocean to the searing hot desert. Some bacteria are harmful, but most are useful and support many forms of life.

Archaea

Archaea look similar to bacteria, but behave very differently. They can survive extreme environments like volcanoes or toxic waste dumps. They are direct descendants of the first organisms on the planet.

'Archaea' is a Greek word meaning 'Ancient things'

Some fungi are used for killing harmful bacteria, and are a key ingredient in some antibiotics.

Fungi

Fungi are made of bigger cells than those of bacteria. Mushrooms, yeasts and moulds are types of fungi. They usually like areas that are warm and damp. They feed off decaying matter and are great at decomposing things.

Viruses

Viruses are the tiniest of microbes. These minuscule particles are not alive. They are 'inanimate complex organic matter'. They have no form of energy and cannot replicate or evolve. They have to hijack other cells in order to reproduce, so are often harmful to humans.

Virus means 'slimy liquid' in Latin.

Sigh.

My name is Demodex and I live on your face!

Microscopic Animals

Microscopic animals are also considered microbes. They have different types of cells just like us. We have lots of microscopic animals on our bodies that we don't even know about.

Protists

Protists are a mixed group of organisms that don't fit into any of the other categories. They have various qualities and serve different purposes – some of which are useful to us and others that are harmful.

This is a PROTIST group

THINK YOU CAN CATEGORISE US?

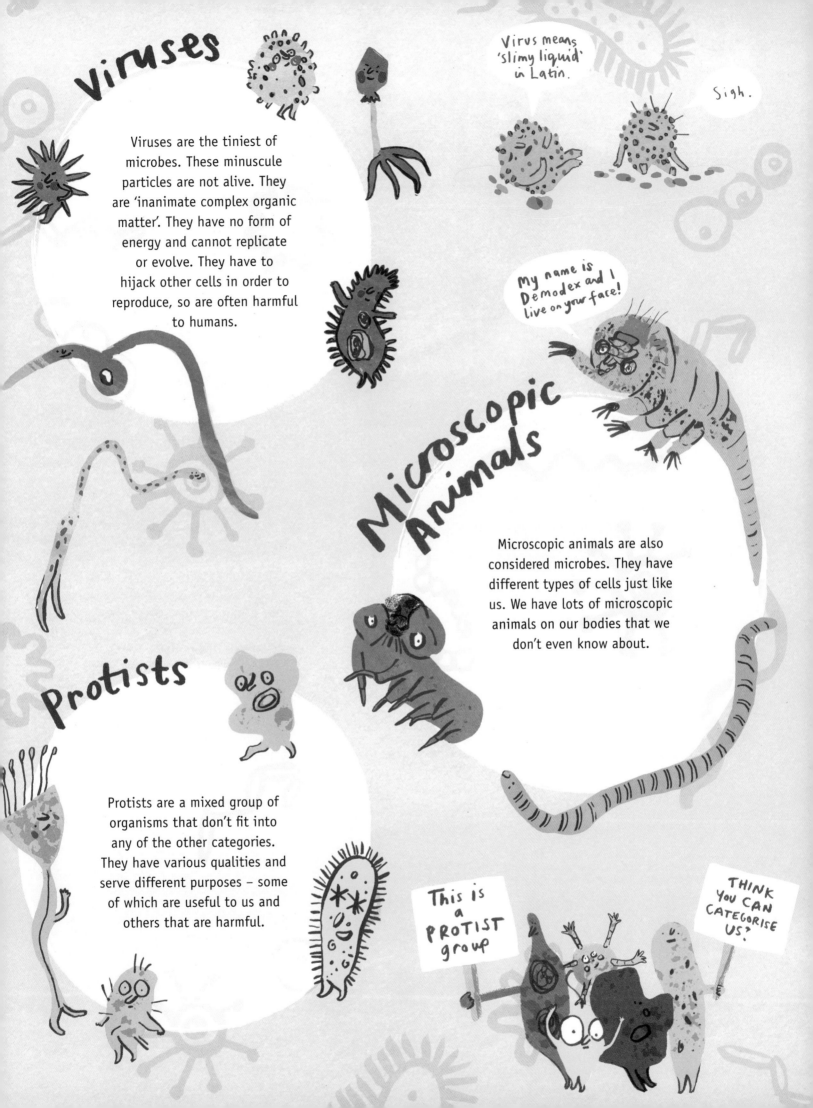

MICROBES IN THE WORLD

Scientists who study these tiny life forms are called microbiologists. They try to understand how microbes live, grow and behave.

These are some of the more extreme microbes that scientists have discovered around the world:

Actually I'm quite big. You can see me under a normal microscope!

TARDIGRADES

These barrel-shaped micro-animals look like eight legged, faceless bears. They can survive boiling or freezing temperatures. If there is no water, they dry up and go into a dormant state from which they can emerge years later.

IDEONELLA SAKAIENSIS

Call me Captain Plastic Fantastic!

This microbe's favourite place is a recycling facility, because it likes to eat certain plastics.

RHIZOBIUM

This bacterium attaches itself onto the root-cells of plants. It takes nitrogen from the air and turns it into nitrates and ammonia that plants can use for food.

And I get a good meal out of it too!

But I also absorb the DNA of things around me so I can evolve.

DEINOCOCCUS RADIODURANS

This is the world's toughest bacterium. It can survive acid, radiation, extreme cold and dehydration.

I'm way tougher than Tardigrade!

BDELLOID ROTIFIERS

Water-dwelling organisms. Like tardigrades, they can dry up when water is scarce and return to life later.

There are no male bdelloid rotifiers! The females lay eggs that are clones of themselves.

IN YOUR BODY

There are microbes on every single thing you touch and eat and even in the air you breathe. And right now inside your body, there are TRILLIONS of microbes. They outnumber your human cells by about 20 percent. In some ways you are more of a home to microbes than you are a person!

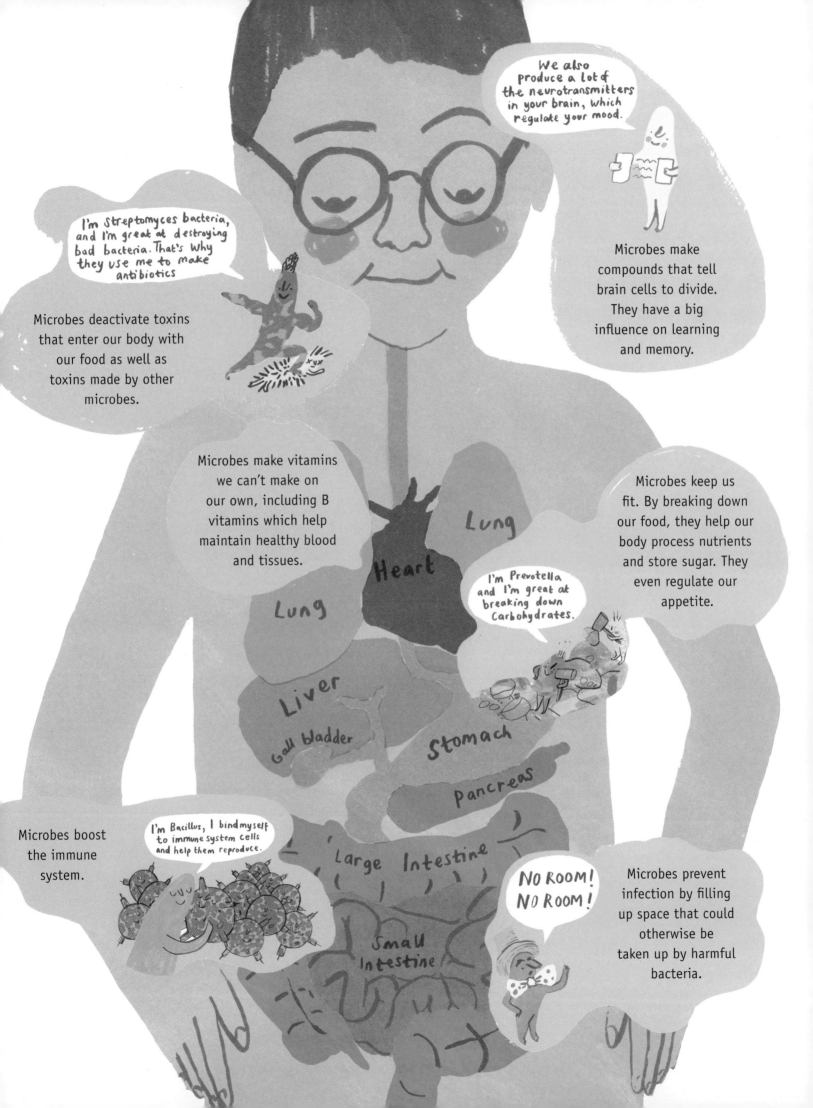

THE BAD GUYS

Not all microbes are good. Some cause infectious diseases like flu and measles.

These bad microbes are called pathogens.

FLU virus

E. Coli Bacterium

LISTERIA Bacterium

MYCOBACTERIUM TUBERCULOSIS Bacterium

SMALL POX Virus

MEASLES Virus

COMMON COLD Virus

Sometimes microbes that are usually 'good' end up multiplying too quickly, or find themselves in the wrong place, and then those microbes can end up doing harm.

It is up to our immune system to protect us against these pathogens!

I'm P. acnes. I live on your skin and keep it moist and smooth. But when I reproduce too quickly, I get stuck in hair follicles and cause acne.

As researchers learn more about microbes, they are beginning to understand how imbalances in microbe populations can cause disease, and how restoring balance can lead to cures.

LET'S LEARN MORE!

When you eat, you are not just eating food, but millions of microbes on and inside the food. And you are not just feeding yourself but all the microbes inside you.

Let's see what happens when we eat food...

OPEN WIDE

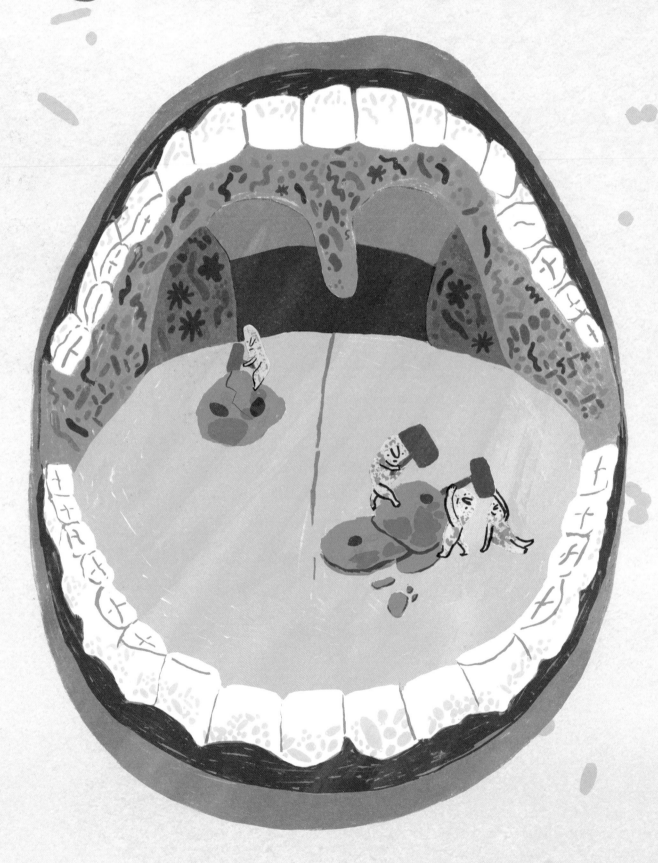

Before you've even swallowed, microbes are hard at work. Chewing turns the food into a lump called a bolus, and the microbes in your mouth and saliva immediately start breaking it down.

Inside your mouth there are over 500 species of microbes. Microbes are adapted to different habitats, so the microbes in your cheek are different to those on your teeth or tongue.

Plaque, that sticky film that forms on our teeth when we don't brush, contains hundreds of species of microbes. Certain types of streptococcus bacteria live on our teeth, breaking down sugar and releasing acid as a by-product. The acid eats through tooth enamel, causing cavities.

Your saliva helps control the bacteria. During the day you'll make a litre of saliva, but at night, your mouth is dryer and bacteria can multiply.

That's why it so important to brush your teeth in the morning!

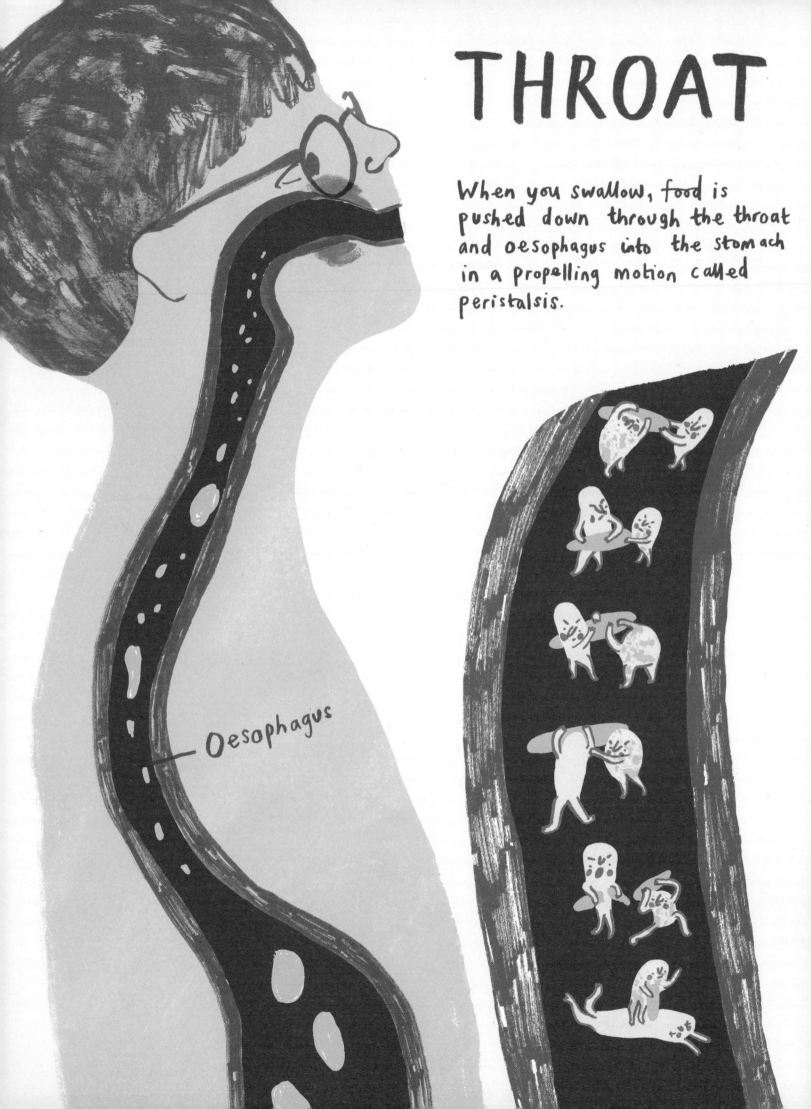

THROAT

When you swallow, food is pushed down through the throat and oesophagus into the stomach in a propelling motion called peristalsis.

Oesophagus

Your tonsils are a fortress, helping to prevent infections. They filter the bacteria and viruses.

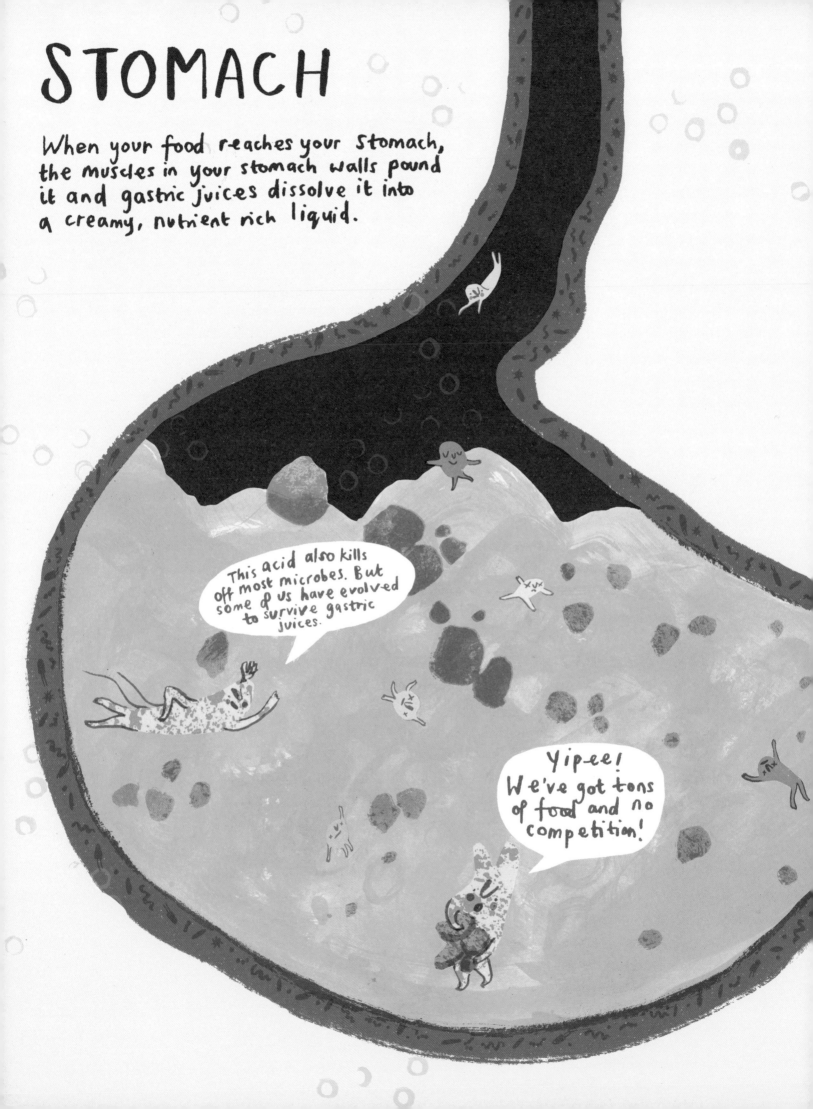

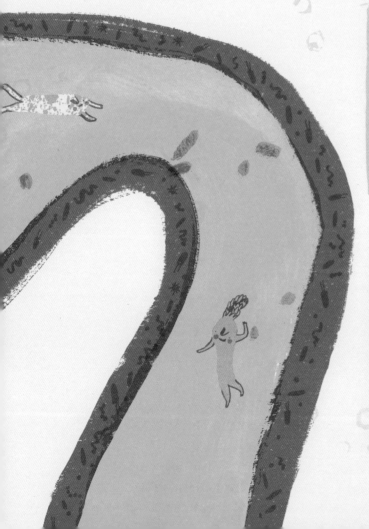

Let's play...
good or evil!

Helicobacter is a sturdy bacteria that can survive the acid of the stomach by hiding inside the stomach lining. It is found in half of all people. Some strains of Helicobacter are dangerous. They can weaken the lining of the stomach and cause ulcers and even cancers!

Evil — definitely evil!

But Helicobacter can also be helpful. Children with Helicobacter are less likely to have asthma, hayfever or eczema, because Helicobacter triggers our immune system and trains it not to overreact to strange microbes like those in pollen.

Hmm, I guess it's a little bit more complicated than I thought!

So... good?

SMALL INTESTINE

The small intestine is a long, winding tube. This is where the vitamins, minerals, carbohydrates, fats and proteins from your food are extracted and passed into your bloodstream.

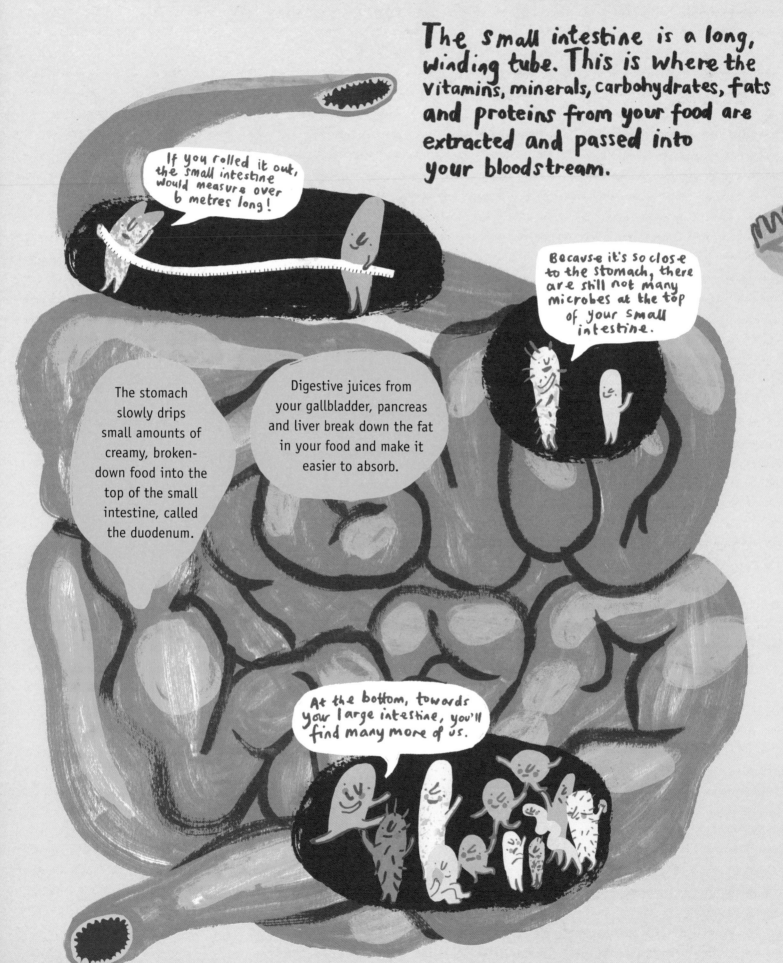

If you rolled it out, the small intestine would measure over 6 metres long!

Because it's so close to the stomach, there are still not many microbes at the top of your small intestine.

The stomach slowly drips small amounts of creamy, broken-down food into the top of the small intestine, called the duodenum.

Digestive juices from your gallbladder, pancreas and liver break down the fat in your food and make it easier to absorb.

At the bottom, towards your large intestine, you'll find many more of us.

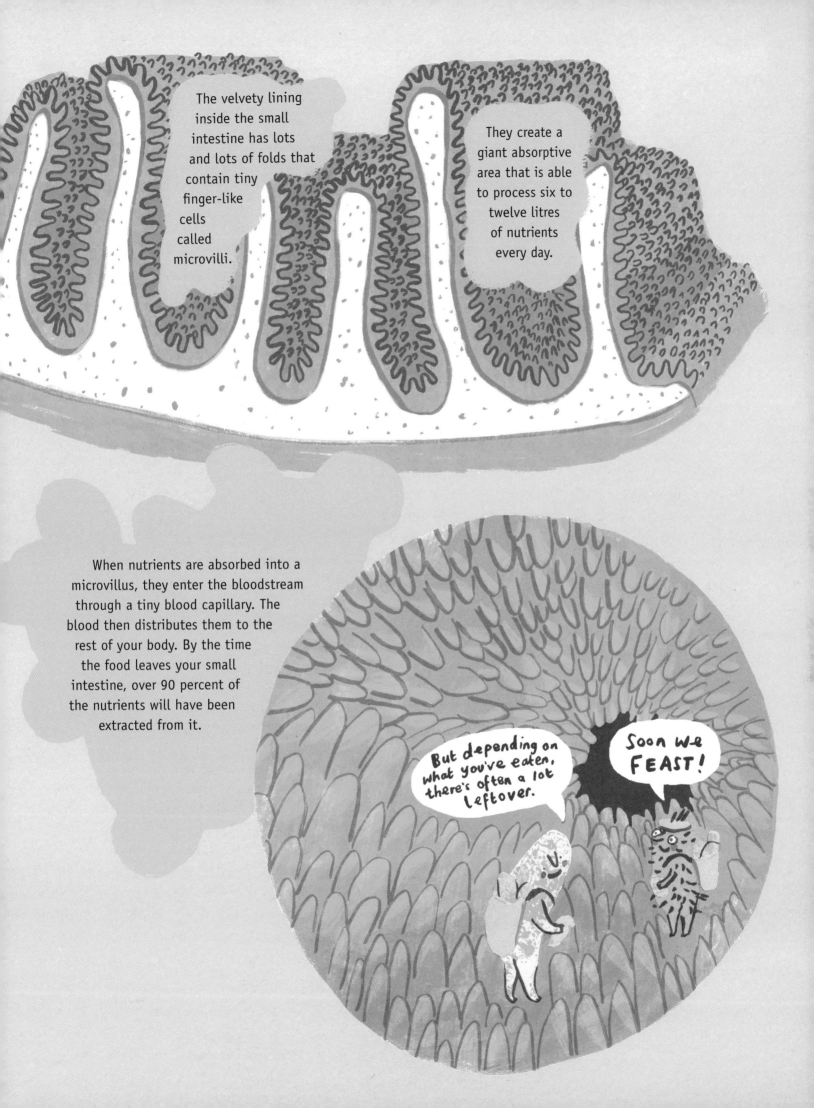

The velvety lining inside the small intestine has lots and lots of folds that contain tiny finger-like cells called microvilli.

They create a giant absorptive area that is able to process six to twelve litres of nutrients every day.

When nutrients are absorbed into a microvillus, they enter the bloodstream through a tiny blood capillary. The blood then distributes them to the rest of your body. By the time the food leaves your small intestine, over 90 percent of the nutrients will have been extracted from it.

But depending on what you've eaten, there's often a lot leftover.

Soon we FEAST!

THE GUT GARDEN

The final part of the digestive process happens in the large intestine – the very heart of the gut garden! Once all the good stuff has been extracted by your body, it's time for the MICROBES to get to work!

90% of us microbes are bacteria

The large intestine is where 99% of your microbes can be found. Not because there are so few elsewhere but because there are SO MANY here!

Welcome to the ~~LARGE INTESTINE~~ GUT GARDEN

The appendix is in the cecum, the first part of the colon. Nobody knows quite what an appendix does, but some scientists believe that it holds a sample of the colon's gut flora, so that it can repopulate the gut after a bad illness or a dose of antibiotics.

Samples call if needed

Ascending Colon

Cecum

Appendix

Rectum

THE ECOSYSTEM INSIDE

Before scientists knew very much about bacteria, they used to think of them as plants, which is why they called the bacteria in our guts 'gut flora'.

That's where we got the name Gut Garden from!

Even though we now know that bacteria are not plants, it is still a helpful metaphor, because our microbiome is an ecosystem of living things, just like a forest or a coral reef.

The species in those environments depend on one another to survive. They compete for food and for space, and they keep each other in check, making sure that one species doesn't overrun the ecosystem. The more types of microbes you have, the richer your ecosystem will be.

Sometimes one species will reproduce too quickly, eating up all the food and killing off the other species in the ecosystem. Other microbes and immune cells need to work hard to restore the balance.

An imbalance in your microbiome is called dysbiosis

HOW DOES YOUR GARDEN GROW?

Everybody has a different ecosystem inside them. Even people in the same family, eating the same diet, have different microbiomes. This is because it's not just diet that affects what lives inside us. Spending time in nature or around pets, or in fact any individual experience can introduce new microbes into your gut.

Children growing up in a house with a dog have been shown to have more diverse microbiomes

When we are in the womb, we are sterile. This means that we have no microbiome at all. The moment we are born, we are colonised by millions of microbes. Over the first two years of our lives, our microbiome changes a lot.

Babies who drink breast milk, for example, will have a microbiome that looks different to that of a formula fed baby, and a baby born via Caesarean will have a different microbiome to a baby born naturally.

At three years old, our microbiome levels out. Things like illness, a change of diet or a course of antibiotics will affect the way our gut garden grows, but it usually returns to a similar landscape to the one that was there before.

IMMUNE SYSTEM

99 percent of your microbes are found in your gut and 80 per cent of your body's immune system is also found in your gut! Coincidence? Not really.

By hanging out with all your bacteria, immune cells learn not to be over-enthusiastic. Instead of just attacking every strange cell that enters the body, they learn to leave the good guys in peace.

IMMUNE

ANTIBIOTICS

Although most bacteria are harmless, some bacteria can cause infections if they are not treated.

DISEASES | BACTERIA | MOULD

The word 'antibiotic' comes from the Greek *anti bios*. This means 'against life'. Antibiotics kill bacteria either by preventing them from reproducing or by stopping them building their cell walls.

Between 1945 and 1972, life expectancy jumped by eight years, thanks to Alexander Fleming's discovery of antibiotics.

Antibiotics kill the bad bacteria that are harming us, but they also kill off the good bacteria. When you take a course of antibiotics, you'll notice that you poo a lot more than usual. A lot of this poo is made up of the dead bacteria from your gut.

PREBIOTICS AND PROBIOTICS

Eating certain prebiotic foods and taking probiotics can help boost our microbiome. But what are they?

PREBIOTIC FOOD is food that is rich in dietary fibre or roughage. This food doesn't digest well in the small intestine, so passes straight through to the gut. Our microbes' favourite food is undigested fibre, and by feeding them, you are also boosting your immune system and helping to regulate your metabolism.

What's good for me is good for you!

Some prebiotic foods are: leeks, asparagus, onions, bananas, flax seeds, wheatbran, oats, apples and garlic.

LOW FIBRE

If you are increasing your fibre intake, do it gradually, or you might end up farting a lot!

PROBIOTICS are 'friendly', live bacteria. The idea is that they pass through our digestive system and improve our microbiome. They usually come in pills or in foods such as yogurt drinks.

LIVE YOGURT

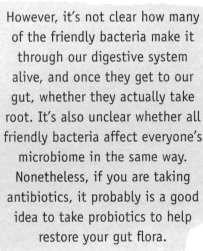

However, it's not clear how many of the friendly bacteria make it through our digestive system alive, and once they get to our gut, whether they actually take root. It's also unclear whether all friendly bacteria affect everyone's microbiome in the same way. Nonetheless, if you are taking antibiotics, it probably is a good idea to take probiotics to help restore your gut flora.

FERMENTATION

When bacteria break down the fibre in your gut, they use a process called fermentation. Fermentation is a way of extracting energy from carbohydrates without the help of oxygen.

A by-product of fermentation is gas, in the form of hydrogen, nitrogen, oxygen, carbon dioxide and methane. Guess what happens when there's a build up of gas in your body...

Time to let one rip! FAAARRRTT

The science of fermentation is called Zymology

SHORT CHAIN FATTY ACIDS

Fermentation produces a by-product called 'short chain fatty acids', which helps regulate your appetite and your energy levels. Scientists found that mice with fewer short chain fatty acids had higher levels of obesity.

Fermentation also happens outside the body.

Fermented food is food that has already been partially digested by microbes before we eat it.

It is a method of preserving food that has been used for many thousands of years.

Some studies indicate that fermented foods can act as a powerful probiotic, helping maintain a healthy immune system.

sauerkraut

Some fermented foods include pickles, sauerkraut, kimchi, miso, kefir, sourdough bread and yogurt.

NATURALLY FERMENTED PICKLES

A lot of fermented foods in supermarkets have been heat treated which kills off all the microbes. Look for the words 'naturally fermented' on the label.

Homemade Sauerkraut

Ingredients
1 medium head of cabbage
2 tbsp. sea salt

1. Shred the cabbage and sprinkle with salt.

2. Put the cabbage in a bowl and pound it with a potato masher until there is enough liquid to cover the cabbage.

3. Stuff the cabbage into a jar, pressing the cabbage underneath the liquid. The cabbage must be completely submerged under the brine, in order for the lactic acid bacteria to grow.

4. Cover the jar with a tight lid or a coffee filter secured with a rubber band and leave it at room temperature for two weeks.

5. Once the flavour is to your liking, put a tight lid on the jar and put it in the fridge. The flavour will continue to develop as it ages.

THE ONLY WAY OUT

The end of your large intestine is called the sigmoid colon. By the time the food has got here, all the nutrients and most of the water have been removed, and what's left is waste material, which solidifies as it moves along.

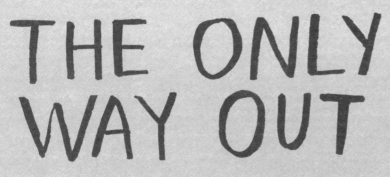

Muscles in the sigmoid colon push the solid waste into the rectum. When the rectum is full, it sends a message to the nerves in the sphincter, which tell the brain that you need to do a poo.

Rectum

Sigmoid colon

When you go to the toilet, the muscles around the bottom of the rectum relax, and your body pushes out the poo using your abdominal muscles.

But what is poo?

Poo is made up of different elements and varies according to diet.

Up to 75 percent of poo is water. This percentage is higher in vegetarians, and lower in people who eat more protein.

I'm Prevotella I'm common in the soft poos of people with high fibre diets.

Up to 25 percent of poo is made of fibre, protein and fats that have not been fully digested.

I'm Ruminococcaceae I'm common in hard poos.

Around 30-50 percent of poo is made of microbes. Our poo is teeming with bacteria, living and dead.

The microbes continue their work even after the waste has left our bodies. This is why animal poo is often used as manure: the microbes work their way into the soil, helping plants to grow.

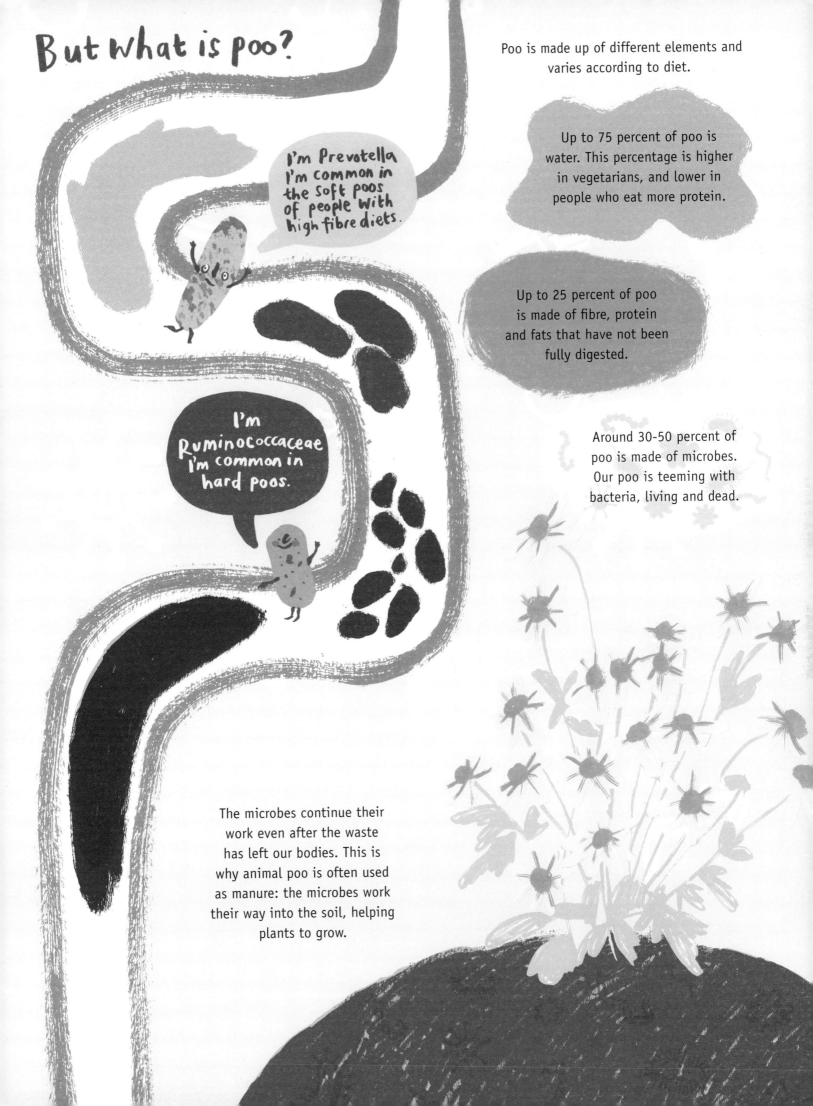

WHEN THINGS GO WRONG

Some people have problems that result from the immune system and the microbiome misreading each other.

Crohns disease happens when a protein that is supposed to prevent microbes from entering the lining of the intestine stops working, and bacteria that should be kept away is allowed in.

Other gut problems arise when the immune system attacks friendly bacteria, causing inflammation.

Another common gut problem results from usually harmless microbes reproducing too quickly. C difficile bacteria is fine in small numbers, but if it multiplies too quickly, it can make a person sick with nausea, diarrhoea and cramps, and it can take a very long time to clear up.

In the case of C difficile, and in certain other gut ailments, scientists are exploring a treatment called Fecal Matter Transplant, or FMT. This means taking the poo of a healthy person, rich with their friendly microbes, and transplanting it into the ill person. In the case of C difficile, this has proven to be very effective as the new microbes quickly overpower the C difficile bacteria.

queue for poo

WHAT NEXT?

The gut microbiome is an exciting new frontier.

Scientists have established that our microbiome boosts immunity, prevents infection, controls our weight and keeps our brains and hormones balanced. They have found links between the microbiome and health problems like multiple sclerosis, diabetes, Parkinson's disease, schizophrenia, cancer and auto-immune diseases.

But they are only just now beginning to examine how the microbiome can be manipulated to prevent or cure these health problems.

One obstacle that scientists face, is that the bacteria inside our gut have evolved to exist within very specific conditions. Unlike the sturdier microbes that live on our skin, gut microbes don't fare well in the lab, dying as soon as they are exposed to air.

Scientists have to rely on experiments on mice in order to work out how certain bacterial imbalances affect health and behaviour.

In the years to come, our understanding of our microbes will be key to resolving all sorts of problems. Imagine that in the future you would only need to gargle with a mouthwash that targets specific bacteria to never have a cavity again!

NOW THIS IS A SPREAD

We humans tend to think that the world was made for our convenience, but microbes vastly outnumber us, dominating life on this planet. In fact if you look at it from that perspective, perhaps we are only here to serve our microbes and provide them with a a comfortable home.

Gut Garden

Written and illustrated by Katie Brosnan
With reference and advice from Dr Deborah
Jessop and Dr Arif Hussain
Design by Studio April

British Library Cataloguing-in-
Publication Data.

A CIP record for this book is available
from the British Library.
ISBN: 978-1-908714-72-5

First published in the United Kingdom
in 2019, and the USA in 2020. This edition
published in 2021 by:
Cicada Books Ltd
48 Burghley Road
London, NW5 1UE
www.cicadabooks.co.uk

Printed in China

About the author

Katie Brosnan achieved an MA
with distinction in Children's Book
Illustration from the Cambridge School
of Art. Katie won a UK prize in the
'Picture This!' competition, 2018, and
was highly commended in the Macmillan
Prize for Illustration. Katie has always
been a little bit short and appreciates
the smaller things in life. She has had a
long-standing fascination with microbes
and their superpowers. When she isn't
drawing or working on books, Katie
helps to run workshops for children
and makes one off ceramic characters.